DEDICATED TO

My parents, Dale and Hazel Parsons. For encouraging my imagination...
My husband Rod and our amazing children and grandchildren. For catapulting me into this
   adventure...
Marty and Leslie Chamberlain, and their powerful impact on my life...
The late Bob Schmidt. For teaching me that nothing is impossible...
Graham Cooke and Andy and Janine Mason. For inspiring and empowering me to pursue my
   dreams...
Heidi Reeves. For her gift of art and for partnering with me to leave a legacy to our future
   generations...

ADVENTURES WITH GRANDMA METTA
WHAT IF?

Written by Jimetta Mayne
Illustrated by Heidi Reeves www.heidireevesart.com
& Katie Nichols
Pagination & Graphic Design by Michelle Sallee
Copyright © 2014 by Jimetta Mayne
ISBN: 978-0-9884992-7-0

 red arrow

Red Arrow Media,
Redding, California

What if?

Adventures with Grandma Metta

by Jimetta Mayne

Illustrated by Heidi Reeves & Katie Nichols

The Adventures with Grandma Metta stories began years ago when my four children were small. Their friends often spent the night, and at bedtime I would tell them all stories. Children are created with beautiful imaginations. Dreaming and pretending are as normal to a child as breathing. I crafted these tales by asking each child to choose a topic or character from his or her imagination. They delighted in the creative process, discovering nothing is impossible.

What's more, they learned they were valuable, brilliant, and able to make good choices. I didn't simply want to tell them about someone else's experience. Every story was specifically designed to expand their imaginations and empower them within real-life situations. My purpose was to take them on a real adventure.

In this story, you will see blank spaces. These are for your children and you to fill in. Everyone gets to contribute, and the story may change each time you read it.

Go beyond the pictures and ask questions that encourage and grant your children permission to dream. Have a conversation, discover what they think, and value their answers (there is no such thing as a wrong answer).

You'll also see what I call the "Ask the Imagination Questions." These are open-ended questions that cannot be answered with a simple "yes" or "no." They activate the ability to think critically and analyze possibilities beyond the illustrations. By encouraging your children to see the "unseen," the "not yet," and the "what could be," they will learn to become problem solvers and long-term thinkers.

Story-time is the perfect opportunity for connection and dream activation between children and adults. Use it well. May your moments together be sweet, like warm berry pie and happy, like a child's anticipation of a birthday surprise.

Jimetta Mayne

Once upon a time _____ , _____ , _____ , and _____ went to visit Grandma Metta at her snug little cabin in the Friendly Woods. Grandma Metta was not their real grandma, but she was so kind and loving, that children from all around Happy Valley loved to spend time with her. And her cabin, nestled amidst tall velvety green pine trees and set by a crystal shimmering lake, was always the backdrop for adventure.

Immediately after a hearty breakfast, the children raced down the well-trodden path to Grandma Metta's cabin. Dressed in her cozy wool sweater, she greeted them with a cheerful wave from her deck.

The children bounded up the steps and gathered around the beautiful old woman whose birdsong voice asked joyfully, "Now, what should we do on such a beautiful day?"

Ask the Imagination!

Where does the story take place?

What is an "illustration"?

What is another name for "the woods"?

What things might you find in the forest?

What is a "cabin"?

What would you like to do in the woods around Grandma Metta's cabin?

Her eyes wrinkled at their edges and twinkled with joy as she made suggestions, "A hike in the woods? A picnic and kites? Perhaps, we will find some berries and bring them back to the cabin to make delicious treats."

Anticipating a delightful day, the children thought about all the fabulous possibilities. Their feet began to itch with the need to run and explore the wonders of the woods.

"Are you ready to go inside and begin gathering food for our picnic?" Grandma Metta asked excitedly.

_____ paused, and looked very serious. "Grandma Metta," she said, "*What if* you don't have what I like? I am a very picky eater."

Grandma Metta smiled knowingly, "Ah, well _____ , *what if* I do have what you like. My pantry and refrigerator are full of tasty foods. Let's not borrow trouble by asking questions like that."

"What does 'borrow trouble' mean?" _____ piped in.

With hands resting on the clean blue and white tile countertop, Grandma Metta answered gently, "It means that we should not try to find a problem if the problem does not exist. So...instead of thinking about what might not be in my pantry, we should be thinking of all the yummy things that are there."

The children nodded and soon the ideas were flying! Sticky peanut butter and jelly, fluffy marshmallow cream, salty turkey, soft bagels with white cream cheese, sweet crumbly cookies, crunchy green apples, bright yellow bananas, and dark purple raisins. Every idea made their taste buds do a happy dance.

Ask the Imagination!

Why do the children
love to come to the cabin?
Who would you invite to Grandma Metta's?
How many children could be at the cabin?
How is a pantry used?
What foods would you like to find in
the pantry?

And soon, scrumptious food lined the counter.

_____ , who liked things neat and clean, saw all of the ingredients piled high and cried out, "Grandma Metta! We are making a big mess."

Grandma Metta grinned, "Sometimes, you have to make a mess to create something wonderful." She paused and tilted her head to the side, continuing thoughtfully, "Like when you paint, sculpt, or garden...Creating often means getting a little messy. But in the end, the result will be worth it, because when we create, we develop precious gifts all of our family and friends can share. Fresh cucumbers from your vegetable patch, a handmade card, beads strung in a pretty pattern, or a song you've practiced over and over. All of them make beautiful love hugs. Creating and loving go hand in hand."

_____ still looked worried. "But *what if* we make a really big mess? What will we do?"

"*What if* we make a gigantic mess? Hmmm... I'll let you answer that. What could we do if we made a serious mess?"

The children took a moment to think. "We could sweep!" said one looking at the floor. " _____ !" suggested another. "And I could put everything away!" finished a third.

Grandma Metta looked pleased, "Those are all good ideas, now let's make lunch!"

Together, they packed a beautiful picnic...and made a mess. But with teamwork, the big mess was quickly and easily cleaned up.

"Now we are ready," Grandma Metta proclaimed, hands on her hips. "Why don't you run upstairs and find a large basket for our lunch?"

Ask the Imagination!

How do you clean up messes?

What are your favorite messy foods to eat?

Who knows what "ingredients" means?

What is another word for "gigantic"?

If you could create your dream picnic, what food would be in it?

11

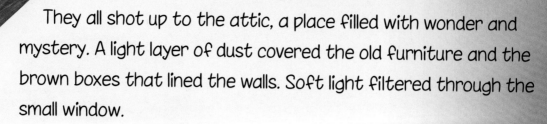

They all shot up to the attic, a place filled with wonder and mystery. A light layer of dust covered the old furniture and the brown boxes that lined the walls. Soft light filtered through the small window.

_____ , who liked things to be organized, looked around at all the stuff in the attic and asked worriedly,

"*What if* we can't find a basket? What will we do?" "*What if* we could come up here and play some rainy afternoon?" _____ asked dreamily, with one hand on the window sill.

Grandma Metta considered each question then replied, "How about we think through both of those *what if's*. One is a problem and one is a possibility. Let's solve the problem first."

"We could use this old hat box!" offered one child pointing to the box. Another held up an old burlap sack, "Or we could use this!"

"What about that _____ ?" Added _____ , motioning towards the wall.

"Look at that, problem solved!" Grandma Metta looked proud. "Now, *what if* we had to stay inside all day? What could we play in the attic?"

Again the children came up with all kinds of brilliant ideas like pretending the attic was a secret cave, reading stories aloud, and building a fort.

"You are each so creative and smart. We don't want any more of those *what if's* taking up precious time and energy. We need it for our adventure! I don't know about all of you, but my stomach is rumbling and I want to go explore on this sunny day. Let's get going!"

Ask the Imagination!

What is an "attic"?
Do you have an attic at your house?
What could you do in Grandma Metta's
attic for a whole afternoon?
How would you feel going into this attic?
What do you think is in your attic?

Ask the Imagination!

What would you do first?
If you could lie on your tummy and look
down into the grass, what would you find?
What things make this a perfect picnic spot?
Where do you think this little squirrel lives?
What foods do you think squirrels eat?

The little expedition tromped deep into the Friendly Woods. They inhaled the sharp tangy scent of pine needles and warm earth. Everything was green and peaceful. Birds chirped softly and the occasional squirrel flitted across the path or looked down from its tree branch perch.

Turning a corner, they suddenly beheld the mother of all picnic spots. It was a beautiful, gentle meadow of soft emerald grass lined with a bubbling, clear creek. Berry bushes sat cheerily beside the water, and to top it off, there was a tire swing!

Grandma Metta spread out the well-worn patchwork quilt (the result of many picnics and cold winter nights keeping little toes warm), and everyone plopped down for lunch. They ate and laughed 'til their hearts and tummies were full.

Before much time had passed, _____ spotted a furry creature in a tree. They reported with distress, "There are squirrels in the bushes! I saw them eating something! *What if* they eat all the berries before we pick them?"

Grandma Metta sat up on her elbows, "Let's solve that *what if* by asking ourselves some questions...Do squirrels eat berries, and if they do, how many could they eat?"

The children took turns guessing. "Five!" "Eleven!" "One thousand berries!"

_____ thought for a minute and then answered slowly, "Well, squirrels are small. Maybe they couldn't eat all the berries."

Ask the Imagination!

What could you do to find your way
back to the picnic spot?
How could you and your friends stick together?
What is another word for "breeze"?
What kind of kite would you like to fly?
What else lives in the sky?

Lying back on the sun-warmed, sweet-smelling grass, Grandma Metta yawned and said, "I think it is time for all of you to go and explore. You can play on the swing, or fly kites in the meadow. There's a perfect breeze today."

The breeze she spoke of swept quietly and gently across their faces. "You could also play in the water. Have fun, then come tell me all about it. But stay nearby–I don't want to lose any of you!"

The children jumped up and took off.

But _____ stayed behind, "Grandma Metta, *what if* I get lost?

"Well, that is a worry. What could you do?"

_____ answered slowly, "I suppose I could find the well-worn path and follow it home...or I could _____ ."

Grandma Metta nodded and chuckled, "And it is always a good idea to stick together. That is a sure way to not get lost. So you better catch up to your friends!"

"I guess I didn't need to worry about that." Then _____ stood up and added with a grin, "That would be 'borrowing trouble,' right, Grandma Metta?"

Grandma Metta beamed, "Exactly! We should be asking, *what if* we have too much fun?"

The warm sun reached higher in the sky, and soon, the children were tired and happy. Dripping wet from playing in the creek, _____ and _____ returned to Grandma Metta who was sitting on the quilt waiting to hear about their adventures. "Well, what did you see?"

"We saw baby chicks, soft, golden yellow and so tiny!" They squealed with delight as they described the newborn birds.

"We also saw _____ ," added _____ . "It was beautiful!"

Just beyond the meadow, Grandma Metta could see large berry bushes spreading out their leafy vines among the trees. She grandly announced that it was time to gather the precious fruit before the sun dipped behind the mountains, and the clean cold evening air swept through the Friendly Woods.

The children carefully cleaned up the picnic and put on their jackets to protect their arms from stickers. Grandma Metta directed the group, "Grab your buckets and fill 'em up!"

Ask the Imagination!

What would it be like to swim with these little chicks?

Where is their mama?

What kind of bird do you think Mama Bird is?

What types of birds do you know?

What would it feel like to hold one of these babies?

What would you do in the creek?

What could you make with berries?

What type of berries do you think are
   in the bushes?

What else could live in the bushes?

What other creatures like to eat berries?

The group dashed down the path into the woods where they found bushes dripping with big ripe berries. Some made it into the buckets and some into their mouths. Slowly, both were filled with the juicy fruit.

"Well, we sure don't have to worry about there being enough berries!" _____ garbled with his mouth full, "There are thousands!"

They picked steadily until the air began to turn chilly and the buckets were heavy. Purple berry juice dripped down every chin. All of their little hands were sticky with berry squish.

"Grandma Metta, _____ began, "My mom says that berries leave a stain. *What if* my face is purple forever?"

"Wouldn't you be a sight!" Grandma Metta couldn't help but giggle. "Well, *what if* we think about ways to get washed up?"

"But there aren't any sinks or bathtubs in the forest," _____ said while looking around.

Together the children considered their surroundings and suddenly they arrived at an answer. "The creek!" they all shouted at once.

Then the children and Grandma Metta washed their hands and faces in the cool water, gathered the quilt and basket and berries, and returned to the cozy cabin to decide what to do with their stash of delicious fruit.

Berry pie was the unanimous treat of choice. They turned the kitchen upside down as they worked together to form buttery crusts and sugary syrup for their fresh berries. But it was worth it—the pies were the best ever. Their warm scent coming from the oven made everyone feel content deep inside.

The children watched the pie emerge from the oven and they were proud of what they made. It had been a truly wonderful day. They had explored the woods, enjoyed a delicious picnic, and saw adorable animals. And to top it all off, they got to devour a berry pie!

When it was time to leave, Grandma Metta smiled and said, "You are so creative at solving *what if's*! I don't think you will ever have to worry about *what if's* when they come around, because you are all brilliant. We'll go on more adventures soon!"

The children did not want their day to end, but they knew they were welcome at Grandma Metta's anytime. Knowing that fact made it easier to return to their homes in Happy Valley. All the children felt powerful and smart enough to solve any *what if's* that might come their way. They waved goodbye and blew kisses to their dear friend in the cozy cabin in the Friendly Woods, promising to come back soon for their next adventure.

Ask the Imagination!

How many pieces of pie are there?

Can you remember some of the animals from the illustrations?

How do you think the children travel home?

What other adventures are Grandma Metta and the children going to have?

TEACHING WITH GRANDMA METTA

`Ask The Imagination` questions are designed to engage students, encourage discussion, and celebrate analytical thinking. Through these sections, teachers can easily assess student understanding and promote participation. *The Adventures with Grandma Metta* series is aligned with the Department of Education standards for Language Arts for students in Kindergarten through 3rd grade.

Key Ideas and Details

- Ask and answer questions: who, what, where, when, why, and how
- Recount stories with a moral, message, or lesson
- Describe how characters in a story respond to events and challenges
- Establish settings and major events in a story, using key details
- Demonstrate a clear theme
- With prompting and support, retell familiar stories, including key details
- With prompting and support, identify characters, settings, and major events
- Ask and answer questions about key details in a text and relate them to other familiar stories

Craft and Structure

- Name the author and illustrator of a story and define the role of each in telling the story
- Ask and answer questions about unknown words in a text
- Identify words and phrases in stories or poems that suggest feelings or appeal to the senses
- Explain major differences between books that tell stories and books that give information
- Identify who is telling the story at various points in a text
- Describe the overall structure of a story from start to finish

Integration of Knowledge and Ideas

- Use illustrations and details in a story to describe its characters, setting, or events
- Describe the relationship between illustrations and the story in which they appear
- Compare and contrast the adventures and experiences of characters in stories to personal knowledge
- With prompting and support, compare and contrast the experiences of characters in familiar stories